Christmas
COMMUNION

SAVORING THE SAVIOR

Alisa Hope Wagner

DEDICATION

This book is dedicated to the unashamed lovers of Jesus Christ who declare His name to the world. May your faith be blessed and multiplied so that all will know the love, grace and mercy of our Lord, Jesus.

I am grateful to my husband, Daniel, and my three kids: Isaac, Levi and Kiki. I pray that the Christmas Spirit adorns your lives like the scent of cinnamon, apples and pine wherever you go.

Also, thank you to my editing team Patricia Coughlin, Holly Smith and Daniel Wagner. May your efforts in this book be rewarded greatly.

"Whoever acknowledges me before others, I will also acknowledge before my Father in heaven" (Matthew 10.32 NIV).

INTRODUCTION

"The Word became flesh and made his dwelling among us. We have seen his glory, the glory of the one and only Son, who came from the Father, full of grace and truth" (John 1.14 NIV).

Finally, the time of God's Son to be born into this world has come! What does Jesus' birth mean for us today? And why does His death and resurrection matter so much? In this *25 Days of Christmas Devotional* about communion, you and your family will discover why the body (bread) and blood (wine) of Jesus Christ are truly the ultimate Christmas gifts to each of us.

Each day allows you to take a sneak peek into the most special Christmas Gift of all. The first five days shine light onto the essentiality of Jesus and His Finished Work on the Cross, and the following twenty days examine the communion elements of bread and wine in preparation for our Christmas Communion. Additionally, every day offers you a *Joy Activity* that will bring Christmas gladness to you, your family and the people you know. As you go through this book, you will begin to live each day with the true Christmas Spirit in your heart.

 At the end of our Christmas journey, two recipes await your arrival. The first recipe is for making homemade bread, which symbolizes the body of Christ. The second recipe is for making homemade grape juice, which symbolizes the blood of Christ. You will be able to make your own Eucharist elements, so you can enjoy Christmas Communion with your family in honor of Jesus' birth.

My prayer is that the beauty of Christmas and the gratitude of Jesus' Finished Work on the Cross will permeate you and your family as an aroma pleasing to God. May you be the delight of our Heavenly Father as you come to know His Son, Jesus, more intimately during this Christmas Season.

> "May God give you heaven's dew and earth's richness— an abundance of grain [Jesus' body] and new wine [Jesus' blood]" (Genesis 27.28 NIV).

Alisa Hope Wagner

DAYS OF CHRISTMAS

December 1

"But he was pierced for our transgressions, he was crushed for our iniquities; the punishment that brought us peace was on him, and by his wounds we are healed" (Isaiah 53.5 NIV).

Jesus was "pierced" and "crushed," so we could have "peace" and be "healed." This is the truth of Christmas. A tiny baby born to make this Great Exchange, like a miracle gift waiting under the Christmas tree to be received and unwrapped by each of us (Romans 3.24-25).

God has called us all to accomplish great things for His glory, but none of us will be expected to take the "transgressions" or sins of the world onto our shoulders. We can rejoice today that, though life may be difficult at times, Jesus was born to accomplish a Great Work on our behalf. Jesus offers us this gift of salvation that no one other than God in the flesh could provide.

How joyful we are that we can receive this gift freely (John 15.11)! The gift of salvation is ours, not because we are good enough, but because God loves us. When all the world tells us that we must be good to earn our Christmas gifts, and if we do something wrong our names are instantly placed on the naughty list, God tells us that no matter what we have done or how badly we have messed up, God's gift of Jesus is totally ours every day. The gift of Jesus is a constant, and it doesn't change!

This gift doesn't care about the color of our skin, the money in the bank or the accomplishments on our wall. It doesn't rely on how we feel, what we know or what we have achieved. This gift is free, given in love and filled to overflowing with God's goodness.

We will learn more about this gift as we get closer to our day of Christmas Communion, and as you walk through each Day of Christmas, remember God's gift of Jesus is free—all you have to do is receive it.

> "For God so loved the world that he gave his one and only Son, that whoever believes in him shall not perish but have eternal life" (John 3.16 NIV).

Joy ACTIVITY

Gift wrap or decorate a shoe box and cut a small opening into the top of the lid. Get a small stack of note cards or cut pieces of paper into squares and place them next to box along with a pen or a pencil. Set the gift box, note paper and pencil in a prominent place in your home.

Over the next twenty-five days, you and your family can fill out little note cards when you see someone doing something special. Or you can fill out a note card when God reveals an aspect of His goodness and love to you. Then on December 25, read the collected notes aloud after your Christmas Communion in a spirit of thankfulness.

December 2

"We all, like sheep, have gone astray, each of us has turned to our own way; and the Lord has laid on him the iniquity of us all" (Isaiah 53.6 NIV).

There are many sins on the Earth that each have their label from bad to worst. However, the root of every sin is found in one choice: to go "our own way." Going our own way means we are going away from God's goodness, provision and protection. Our desire to go our own way is why Jesus was born. God gave us free will to create beauty for His glory, but He also knew we would use our free will to go astray at times. The Christmas Gift of salvation through the cross gives us a double-fold blessing. First, all of our sins are wiped clean. They are no longer seen on Earth or in Heaven. Second, what we create and accomplish in obedience to God is pleasing to Him. Our imperfect offerings to God are now perfect in God's eyes.

Our lives on Earth matter. We have value and purpose, and God has a destiny for each one of us (Romans 8.28). We will never be able to achieve this destiny without God's grace. Truly, we will never be perfect, but we can be faithful. We have so much joy because of the salvation we have through Jesus Christ. As long as we accept this Great Gift, we don't have to fret over our mistakes. Knowing that we have a loving God who rejoices over us should give us the courage to chase after all our God-given dreams.

Moreover, the value that we each carry will overflow onto the people around us. They should sense a joy about us that can't be quenched by external circumstances. The love we receive from God through Jesus Christ is abounding, and if we let it, will pour out into our hearts, spilling over onto our relationships, actions and lives. We can rejoice each day because we are loved by a loving God!

Joy ACTIVITY

Three is a special number because it represents the Trinity: God the Father, God the Son and God the Holy Spirit. God the Father created us with value and purpose. God the Son died for us and prays for us continuously. And God the Holy Spirit dwells within us and guides us. One God who interacts with His people in three different ways.

You too interact with people in at least three different ways, as well. You may be a parent, a son or daughter, a student, a boss, an employee, a customer or even a servant. Today, bless three people in a special way.

You can pay for someone's coffee. Bring a teacher a note or a gift. Wash your parent's car or take your spouse on a date. You have value on this Earth to make a difference in people's lives. Bless three people and watch for the smiles and hugs you receive for taking a moment to impart worth onto them. Your act of kindness will not only brighten someone's day; it will also spread the Christmas Spirit.

December 3

"Bear with each other and forgive one another if any of you has a grievance against someone. Forgive as the Lord forgave you" (Colossians 3.13 NIV).

Forgiveness is one of the biggest truths about Jesus' birth. He was born in the manger in order to forgive the world. His gift of salvation is the most beautiful, meaningful and life-changing present of all. Because of Jesus' forgiveness, we can now have a relationship with a Holy God. Not only that, we can have God's Spirit, the Holy Spirit, living inside of us, guiding and comforting us each day.

Although forgiveness can often times be easy to receive, other times it may be difficult to extend. People are not perfect. They can hurt us and hurt  those we love. However, the Bible is clear. God wants us to forgive others as He has forgiven us through the Finished Work of Jesus Christ (Ephesians 4.32). Forgiving others is like pulling out the thorn of bitterness that will start an infection in our soul if we ignore it. Forgiveness allows us to let go of our pain and shame and give them both to God.

We have been given the Greatest Gift— Jesus' forgiveness for all our past, present and future sins. This truth can help us overcome our hurt when we are wounded by others. If we can forgive, God can and will comfort our souls and heal our wounds. Forgiveness is the seed that produces a life abundant with joy, peace and hope.

Joy ACTIVITY

Has someone hurt you or someone you love lately? Are you carrying the weight of unforgiveness? God is waiting for you to give Him the seed of forgiveness, so He can bless you with a harvest of His peace. You may feel entitled to hold onto the unforgiveness, but God has something so much better to give you. But first you must free your hands of carrying your bitterness, so they can embrace His blessings.

Do a little soul-searching and see if you have been harboring unforgiveness. If so, make an opportunity today to offer forgiveness to the person who has hurt you. If you do not have contact with that person, write a little note letting them know that you forgive them. You can bury the note, place it in a fireplace or give it to a trusted friend.

Finally, if the one you are having trouble forgiving is yourself, you must do that today.

Withholding forgiveness from yourself is just as harmful as withholding it from someone else. Trust that the cross is much stronger than your mistakes. Jesus died to free you from condemnation (John 3.17). Forgive yourself, so you can walk confidently in the freedom of grace.

December 4

"And the Holy Spirit descended on him in bodily form like a dove. And a voice came from heaven: "You are my Son, whom I love; with you I am well pleased" (Luke 3.22 NIV).

We find in Luke 3.22 a single verse that encompasses our Triune God. We read about the Holy Spirit coming down like a dove. We read about God's voice speaking from Heaven. And we read about Jesus Christ getting baptized. Before our eyes, we see the Trinity all at the same place on Earth. One God Who is expressing Himself in three different ways to a world and people He loves.

God is not some distant perfect Being looking from the clouds down at His creation. Through the Person of Jesus Christ, God walked this Earth. His sandaled feet became dirty on dusty roads. He ate. He slept. He wept. He laughed. And He died. He led a perfect life submitted to God as a demonstration to us that we are not alone. We have a God that not only created us and cares for us but also understands us.

Jesus knows what we are going through. The Bible says He was tempted in every way, so He understands firsthand about our struggles, heartache and hurts (Hebrews 4.15). This is why He is our Great Intercessor (Romans 8.34). He knows exactly what to pray. Jesus is God's gift to us, letting us know that He is with us every step of the way. We can overcome all obstacles, believing that we are not alone. And when our bodies die, we don't have to be scared because Jesus has arrived in Heaven first, and He waits to greet us with open arms when we arrive.

Joy ACTIVITY

You are not alone! Jesus walked this Earth and touched many people's lives along the way, and He is still supernaturally touching lives today. Choose one of the Gospels of the Bible – Matthew, Mark, Luke or John—and get to know your Savior. Pick a section of verses between His birth and death where Jesus interacted with people.

Read these verses aloud and examine how Jesus talked, interacted and responded to the people He loved and died for. Once you are done reading, offer up a prayer to God and thank Him for sending His Son, Jesus, to Earth, so you wouldn't have to walk this life alone. Let God know how thankful you are that He is our Triune God, and He knows exactly what it feels like to walk in an imperfect world according to God's perfect plan.

December 5

"No one takes it from me, but I lay it down of my own accord. I have authority to lay it down and authority to take it up again. This command I received from my Father" (John 10.18 NIV).

When we reflect on Jesus' birth, we rejoice because He is God's gift to the world. But as it is with all life, we know that death is on the other end of birth. Jesus understood that He would be giving His life as payment for our sins, and He gave His life willingly. However, He also knew that death would not have the ultimate victory. Jesus gave His life, but He had the authority to "take it up again."

When we accept Jesus as our Lord and Savior, the Bible says we are buried and raised to life in Him (Romans 6.4). So our story in Christ doesn't end in death either! We have been born in flesh, which leads to death. But we have also been born in the spirit, which leads to eternal life (John 3.5). We celebrate Christmas knowing that the birth of a tiny baby would free us from the sting of death (1 Corinthians 15.55-57).

 Therefore, Christmas truly is something to celebrate. We decorate our homes. We wrap gifts. We make cookies. We sing carols. And we spread goodwill because of our overwhelming joy in the knowledge that death doesn't have the final word. Jesus Christ has authority over death, and He happily and freely gives this authority to us. Jesus has the final word, and He declares "life" over all of us. The birth of Jesus is the heart of Christmas, and our joy in this Gift

can't help but permeate every aspect of our daily life.

Joy ACTIVITY

The Christmas traditions we have grown accustomed first began as outpourings of a rejoicing heart. Sometimes, we can get caught up in our traditions and forget the root of why we do them. God cares more about the motives behind our Christmas traditions than the traditions themselves. This Christmas Season, choose one of your Christmas traditions and do it out of a rejoicing heart, overwhelmed by God's gift of Jesus.

Bake cookies for a neighbor, letting them know how grateful you are for God's Son. Wrap a gift for a friend, rejoicing that you have been sealed in Jesus' love. Decorate your Christmas tree as a declaration of your awe of God's gift. Watch your Christmas traditions overflow with thankfulness and wonder simply by placing the focus on Jesus.

December 6

"And when he had given thanks, he broke it and said, 'This is my body, which is for you; do this in remembrance of me.' In the same way, after supper he took the cup, saying, 'This cup is the new covenant in my blood; do this, whenever you drink it, in remembrance of me'" (1 Corinthians 11.24-25 NIV).

N ow that we know that Jesus is the true meaning of Christmas, we will take the next twenty days to look at Jesus in light of the communion elements: Bread and Wine. Understanding the importance of each element in regard to how they reflect Jesus and His Finished Work on the Cross will fuel our Christmas Communion experience with power and belief. Before we begin, we must first understand the importance of a metaphor.

A metaphor helps us to understand abstract themes in concrete ways. A metaphor compares two unlike things to make a unique comparison. Jesus is compared to many things: Lamb, Light, Shepherd, Bridegroom, Rock, the Word, Bread and Wine. Each of these metaphors shines light on abstract, powerful truths about our Lord and Savior.

Jesus is our Bread, which is His Body broken on our behalf. Jesus is our Wine, which is His Blood poured out on our behalf. These two metaphors are so important to Jesus that they became the theme of His Last Supper with His disciples before He was crucified. Why are these two metaphors so important? We will discover the truth about their transforming power by the end of the book just in time for our own communion.

Combining the Christmas season with communion will give us a beautiful "remembrance" that will flood our Christmas season with an overflowing joy for God's Great Gift to us. This joy will become our key to claiming gratitude during difficult times, healing in painful times and peace in stressful times. Our joy will spread beyond the Christmas season as we discover that the gift of Jesus is ours every day.

Joy ACTIVITY

There are many metaphors for Jesus in the Bible. Can you think of a few more metaphors that describe Who He has been for you this year? Has he been your Doctor, healing your wounds? Your Lawyer, pleading your case? Your Bodyguard, protecting your family? Or your Best Friend, sharing your journey?

Reflect on who and what Jesus has been for you this season. Write down your metaphor and explain what His presence has meant to you. Pray back your written words to God, letting all of Heaven know that Jesus has been exactly what you needed.

December 7

"And he directed the people to sit down on the grass. Taking the five loaves and the two fish and looking up to heaven, he gave thanks and broke the loaves. Then he gave them to the disciples, and the disciples gave them to the people. They all ate and were satisfied, and the disciples picked up twelve basketfuls of broken pieces that were left over" (Matthew 14.19-20 NIV).

Thankfulness and brokenness. How could these two things go hand in hand? But that is exactly what was needed for Jesus to multiply the loaves of bread, so the multitude could be fed. Jesus gave thanks for the loaves and then He broke them. After

 being broken, they became a supernatural supply of sustenance for the desperate, hungry people in the wilderness. They had more than enough, and the disciples picked up twelve baskets filled with leftovers.

Brokenness is a beautiful process when done in the careful hands of God. Just like a seed must be broken in the Earth in order to produce many seeds (John 12.24), we must go through a season of brokenness in order for God to produce His seeds of blessings within us. Brokenness can lead to one of two things: bitterness or blessing. The fork in the road for these two opposing paths begins with thankfulness. When we thank God even in the hard times, we show Him that we trust Him and that we believe that there are no hopeless endings with Him.

God can do His supernatural work through our brokenness when it is offered up to Him in thanksgiving. Just like the bread, Jesus' body was broken for us, so His supernatural grace could be multiplied to the far reaches of the Earth. Not only will God's grace satisfy us, there will be leftovers that can be gathered through our faithfulness. Trust God with your life. Know that He will multiply His blessings through your brokenness. And remember, you are not alone. Jesus was broken like bread, and now Heaven has been made available to us all.

Joy ACTIVITY

Have you been in a season of brokenness? Were you able to trust God with the pieces of our life, knowing that His supernatural power would multiply blessings in your vulnerability? If you are going through a difficult season now, will you try to offer your thankfulness to God, believing that there are no hopeless endings through Jesus?

Image yourself in the wilderness with Jesus and the multitude. He lifts up a loaf of bread that symbolizes your life. He raises the bread up and gives thanks to God. Then He takes the bread and breaks it. It hurts for the moment, but then a supernatural transference takes place. Within your brokenness, Jesus' blessings can multiply— not only to you and your family but to the multitude surrounding you, as well.

December 8

"And the master of the banquet tasted the water that had been turned into wine. He did not realize where it had come from, though the servants who had drawn the water knew. Then he called the bridegroom aside and said, 'Everyone brings out the choice wine first and then the cheaper wine after the guests have had too much to drink; but you have saved the best till now'" (John 2.9-10 NIV).

Jesus' first public miracle was turning water into wine at the wedding of Cana. There are many implications of this demonstration but let us look at the two elements: water and wine. The first time water poured onto the Earth, everything died except Noah and his family who were protected in the Ark (Genesis 7.23). Water represents the Living Spirit of God, and none of us is worthy to stand under the holiness of these divine floods. We would all be wiped out, which is why God promised to never flood the Earth again, giving the sign of His rainbow in the sky (Genesis 9.11).

 However, Jesus was born into our Earth, carrying the Living Water in the Ark of His body. He became, Immanuel, God with us, so He could bring Living Water to the world without harming it. The hallowed water of God was transformed into wine through the Person of Jesus Christ. Wine is symbolic of water mixed with Earth, forming fruit that humans can consume. The fruit of the vine is in essence fleshed covered Living Water poured out to the world. No flood. No death. Only supernatural wine engulfing the Earth, making salvation available to anyone who thirsts (John 4.14).

Joy ACTIVITY

Jesus uses another metaphor in the Bible, calling Himself the Vine (John 15.5). He says if we remain in this vine, we will produce many fruits. But if we separate from this vine, we can do nothing. Are there any areas of your life that seem fruitless? Pick one of those areas and ask yourself if you have removed it from the Vine of Christ. If you know it is rooted in Christ, then you must trust that there is fruit, but it hasn't manifested in the physical world yet.

However, if you know that this area is not submitted to Christ, will you ask forgiveness from God for not trusting Him with that area? Get a piece of paper or grab your journal. Draw a winding vine across the page and create circles along that vine, representing those things that are submitted to God. Finally, draw the circle that represents the area you have withheld from God. Label that fruit with your area as a symbol that you are now plugging it back into the Vine of Christ.

December 9

"Then Jesus declared, 'I am the bread of life. Whoever comes to me will never go hungry, and whoever believes in me will never be thirsty'" (John 6.35 NIV).

Whether we believe it or not, there is an innate desire in us to know and be known by our Creator. God has planted Heaven in our DNA, and there is no escaping it (Ecclesiastes 3.11). People are looking for value and meaning, and when they are not discovered, they will try to distract themselves with lesser, fleeting things of this Earth. Jesus calls Himself the Bread of Life, which is the only God-given nourishment that will satisfy our hunger for meaning and purpose. This Bread is a tangible manifestation on Earth of what is unseen in the spiritual realm. This Bread is God in the Flesh, given to the world in the only way He can be received by us—through His Son, Jesus Christ.

Jesus said that "Blessed are those who hunger and thirst for righteousness, for they will be filled" (Matthew 5.6 NIV). We are blessed when we see our hunger and thirst. We are blessed when we see our need for a Savior. Only when we hunger will we ask and be filled. When we don't see our need and don't feel our hunger, we will never reach out for something more. We will be content with the petty value the world can offer and the small amount of meaning the world can give us. But the world's food is bankrupt of eternal nutrients, and it will never satisfy our innate desire to have eternal value.

The Bread is a metaphor of a supernatural and eternal purpose that we can only achieve through Christ. God has so much goodness that He wants to give us. The Bible says to "Taste and see that the Lord is good…" (Psalms 34.8 NIV). Tasting the goodness of God is impossible on our own. However, Jesus came into this Earth to be our Bread of Life, and He is available to all who hunger for Him.

Joy ACTIVITY

Is there a place in your life in which you hunger but you have no way to satisfy it? Instead of looking for external ways to quench your appetite, look to Jesus. He is the Bread of Life and His sustenance is always ready to satisfy a hungry soul. Many times the answer to our hunger is within us, as we lean into a deeper relationship with the Lord. He wants you to consume more of His goodness, and He will limit outside sources in order to get you to look to Him.

Find a bread product in your home. Sit with your Bible and the bread, praying to God and asking Him to reveal areas of your life in which you hunger. Ask God to satisfy this hunger. Because of Jesus' Finished Work on the Cross, God's Spirit lives within you. You have the Fruits of His Spirit available to you at any time, so ask and receive from this spiritual harvest (Galatians 5.22-23 NIV). Below is a list of God's Fruit. As you read each one, take a bite of the bread as a symbol that you are accepting this Fruit from Jesus.

- Love
- Joy
- Peace
- Forbearance
- Kindness
- Goodness
- Faithfulness
- Gentleness
- Self-control

December 10

"In him we have redemption through his blood, the forgiveness of sins, in accordance with the riches of God's grace" (Ephesians 1.7 NIV).

The wine is a metaphor of Jesus' blood. Because of gruesome movies, books and other misguided works of art, the blood has become a negative image in our society today. However, blood is the life essence of a living thing. It is not an ugly image; rather, it is the image of the material DNA of a unique creation. Jesus' blood has an even more awesome relevancy to it. Jesus is God in the flesh, so His blood is the essence of God on Earth. This is why the blood of Christ is so powerful. It is powerful enough to redeem the world of all sins and reconcile the entire Earth back to God.

Jesus' blood is poured out in the New Covenant where a single sacrifice of God's only Son would forgive the sins of the world. Now we can have the promised Holy Spirit even in a world still affected by sin (John 14.6).

We drink from the blood of Jesus, knowing that the Resurrection Power of the Cross transforms us into children of God and co-heirs with Christ (Romans 8.17), and we become a royal and holy priesthood who walk in the light of God (1 Peter 2.9). The blood of Jesus is a flood of grace that washes over the world, making everything pleasing to God. Sin no longer has the final word. Jesus allowed His body to be broken, so His blood would pour out in a New Covenant of grace.

Joy ACTIVITY

In the Old Covenant based on law rather than grace, the sacrificial lamb was offered and the priest would dip his finger in the blood and sprinkle it on the altar (Leviticus 3.2). This sprinkled blood would purify and redeem whatever it touched. Identify an area of your life that needs to be purified and redeemed. If you have accepted Jesus as your Lord and Savior, this area has been washed by the blood, but sometimes it's hard to believe by faith when our physical eyes don't see a change.

Imagine the blood of Jesus sprinkled over this area, this person or this situation. Don't be disgusted by the blood; instead, realize that the blood is the essence of God pouring over you, your loved one and your situation. Thank God for giving His Son, so He could wash your life with His goodness and grace.

December 11

"But here is the bread that comes down from heaven, which anyone may eat and not die. I am the living bread that came down from heaven. Whoever eats this bread will live forever. This bread is my flesh, which I will give for the life of the world" (John 6.50-51 NIV).

Bread is symbolic of our basic need for human survival. Bread was made up of crushed grain and mixed with a little oil and water. Then it was baked, providing the consumer with the energy to finish the day's work. Jesus came to Earth to show the world that humans are not merely physical beings. There is also a spiritual aspect of our reality that is even more important. Just like our body hungers for physical survival, our spirits hunger too for eternal survival. We are body and spirit, and both crave to not only survive, but to thrive.

And since it is our spirits that continue forever, their health is essential to a fulfilling and purposeful life on Earth. As we age, our bodies show the signs of wear and tear. However, our spirits are ageless because they are eternal. They are forever young with the veracity to thrive no matter how old we look on the outside.

Jesus says that anyone who eats of His bread will never die. This physical bread is a supernatural metaphor of what Jesus alone can give us. He alone is the Bread of Life, and He offers this bread to us freely. He waits with His arms reaching out to give us this bread, which is His body broken for the world's redemption. We only need to take this bread and eat. Once we eat of God's sustaining bread to us through Jesus Christ, our spirits will revive with a desire for more of God's presence.

Joy ACTIVITY

O nce we take the first bite of Jesus' bread, we have eternal life with Him in Heaven. This bread represents His body that was given to us for our reconciliation back to God—a free gift that we cannot earn or deserve. However, the feast doesn't end there. Jesus says in the Bible that He came to not only give us life but to give us life abundantly (John 10.10).

Imagine you are sitting at a table. Jesus is at the head of the table, and He is presenting you with dozens and dozens of loaves of bread. The loaves are all different shapes, sizes, colors, scents and textures; and they each have what you need at different times in your life. Now look at your current situation and pinpoint an area that you lack abundance. Ask Jesus which loaf of bread will supply your need in that area. Identify the bread and grab it in your hands—then feast, trusting that God is providing exactly what you need with His overwhelming abundance.

December 12

"How much more, then, will the blood of Christ, who through the eternal Spirit offered himself unblemished to God, cleanse our consciences from acts that lead to death, so that we may serve the living God!" (Hebrews 9.14 NIV).

God created Heaven and Earth, animals and humans, during the first six days of creation, and they were all pleasing to Him (Genesis 1.31). However, He created us in His image giving us free will, so we could be creative, free-thinking sons and daughters. With our free will, God knew we would sin and make mistakes, which is why He also gave us His Son, Jesus Christ. God rested on the seventh day of creation, knowing Jesus would be Lord over the Sabbath, spilling His blood to reconcile our broken world back to God (Matthew 12.8).

We live in the New Testament era where the blood of Jesus has been sprinkled over the Earth. We drink wine or juice as a reminder of Jesus' blood that has been poured out to cleanse us and the Earth from the blemishes caused by sin. Through the lens of the blood, God sees His perfect creation once more, and we are pleasing to Him. Moreover, every day is pleasing to Him. We recognize this spiritual truth as we taste the fruit of the vine.

It may be difficult to comprehend that we have been cleansed from all the stains of sin. Many times, our conscience wants to hold onto sin because that is what our eyes see. However, as we align our perspective with God's perspective, we will see that the blood of Jesus Christ has supreme authority, and everything must bow to His power (Philippians 2.10). The blood of Jesus that spilled out from His broken body on the cross is the seed of redemption that has multiplied throughout the Earth. No sin will ever be stronger than the blood (wine) and the bread (body) of Christ, given to us as the ultimate Christmas Gift.

Joy ACTIVITY

Juice is the part of the fruit with the most water. Juice has all the properties of the fruit, with its abundance of vitamins and nutrients, flowing freely in liquid form. Juice must have a container in which to hold it. The Bible calls us jars of clay, which can hold the treasure of Jesus Christ within us (2 Corinthians 4.7). We are literally the containers for which Jesus' redeeming blood can fill.

Pick any fruit from your refrigerator— orange, pineapple, strawberry, blueberry or lemon. Set a cup on the counter and squeeze the essence of the fruit into the cup. Do you see how the juice leaves the fruit and flows into the container? That is what Jesus has done for you. He allowed His body to be crushed, so His blood could pour God's goodness into your life (Isaiah 53.5). As you watch the juice flowing, recognize that Jesus' blood is flowing into your life, healing, redeeming, refreshing and rejuvenating every area you allow it to touch.

December 13

"Jesus answered, 'It is written: "Man shall not live on bread alone, but on every word that comes from the mouth of God"'" (Matthew 4.4 NIV).

Our spirits crave sustenance that only God can give us through the Gift of Jesus Christ. We desire purpose, meaning, unconditional love and to be part of an eternal story. One of the best ways we can receive sustenance from God is through His written Word, the Bible. Both the Old and New Testaments point to the birth and sacrifice of Jesus, so God's manifest glory could explode through space and time.

In the Old Testament, a sacrifice was needed to wash away the sins of God's People

(Leviticus 4.2). And in the New Testament, John the Baptist declared: "Look, the Lamb of God, who takes away the sin of the world!" (John 1.29 NIV). Jesus would fulfill God's holy standard on our behalf, so we could have a relationship with Him. The Bible is filled with real-life stories that testify to God's love, goodness, perfection and miraculous provision.

As we consume God's Word, we feed on the Bread of Life and our hunger for God is both awakened and satisfied. To some people, the Bible looks like nothing more than historical documents. However, with the Holy Spirit inside of us through the Finished Work of Jesus Christ, our minds and hearts are opened to the supernatural flow of the Bible. Indeed, the "...word of God is alive and active..." (Hebrews 4.12 NIV). As we read, the Person of Jesus provides us with everything we need each day to live in His peace, provision and love.

Joy ACTIVITY

Plan ahead. The year is coming to an end, and you can begin the new year with a daily devotional or a one-year Bible. Take a trip to your favorite Christian bookstore or do a search online and ask the Holy Spirit to lead you to exactly what He wants you to read. There are thousands of amazing books, and God knows the one you will be needing each day for the next year. As you "eat" from your daily slice of God's Word, you'll be amazed how God speaks to you each day.

If you would like a suggestion, I have published an award-winning one-year devotional, entitled, _Slay the Day: Your Daily Dose of Victory_. Each day is about a five-minute read, and the book covers every book of the Bible. You can follow along in God's Word and see what else He brings to you during your reading time. You can purchase this book on Amazon.

December 14

"And through him to reconcile to himself all things, whether things on earth or things in heaven, by making peace through his blood, shed on the cross" (Colossians 1.20 NIV).

Jesus' blood reconciles us back to God. Adam and Eve sinned in the Garden of Eden; which caused us to be separated from God, but now through Jesus, we are brought back into relationship with God (1 Corinthians 15.22). The blood of Jesus is God's purifying essence cleansing the world with His holiness. God's creations are always perfect and loved. However, He gave us free will, so we could choose to love Him back. With that free will we make mistakes, which causes us to lose our perfection. But now through Jesus' blood and God's grace, we can now be perfect and loved once more.

God's perfection has been fulfilled on our behalf through the perfect sacrifice of Jesus. Jesus took our sins and gave us His righteousness, so now God can embrace us as perfect creations once more. According to Merriam-Webster Dictionary, reconcile means "to restore friendship."

Our relationship with God is broken by sin, but Jesus restored it with His blood. The wine or juice we drink during communion symbolizes this restored relationship. As we drink, we receive a fresh understanding and revived thankfulness of the Great Gift God has given us. Praise God! We never have to be alone. God is with us each day because of the sacrifice of Jesus on the cross!

Joy ACTIVITY

Sometimes we don't recognize the gift of never being alone. God is with us every moment of every day. He sticks with us through the good times and the hard times. His strength is ours during difficult times. His peace is ours during stressful times. His joy is ours during fun times. And His provision is ours during times of need.

The Christmas season can often be hectic. Sometimes, we are so busy running around that we forget to spend time with God and receive what He wants to give us this day. Take time today to talk with God. Go for a walk. Hide in your closet. Sit on the porch. Whatever you do, spend time with God. Tell Him your thoughts and feelings and wait for Him to speak back or impart a sense of His presence to you.

December 15

"This, then, is how you should pray: 'Our Father in heaven, hallowed be your name, your kingdom come, your will be done, on earth as it is in heaven. Give us today our daily bread. And forgive us our debts, as we also have forgiven our debtors. And lead us not into temptation, but deliver us from the evil one'" (Matthew 6.9-13 NIV).

Many times our thoughts are in the future. We allow fear and worry to consume today over what we don't have to face until tomorrow. Jesus said for us to pray, "Give us today our daily bread." That means God will only give us the bread (nourishment and provision through Christ) for what we need to be successful today.

He's not going to give us the bread for what we need be successful tomorrow, next week or next month. We build our faith when we learn to rely on God without knowing the full picture of His provision.

The Bible says to capture every thought that is not aligned with God (2 Corinthians 10.5). Worry, fear, guilt, envy and mistrust are not of God and should instantly be captured and demolished. When our eyes are on today, and God's provision at this very moment, we will alleviate the mounting stress that seeks to build in our minds. God loves us. He wants to provide for us, but He also wants us to trust Him with our lives and situations. He has the bread ready for us when we need it, so we can let go of worry and have faith that God will provide at just the right time.

Find a stone for each worry that is weighing you down. Be as creative or simplistic as you want. You can paint the stones or use a marker to simply write on them. Write a future worry on each stone that you have been carrying. Once you are done marking or painting your worry stones, take the stones outside and leave them on  your porch. Every time you pass these stones, give a quick prayer of trust to God that they are in His capable hands.

Besides your prayer, you should no longer be thinking about these worries (Matthew 6.34). When God provides for one of your worries, go back to the pile of rocks and remove that stone. Thank God for providing just what you need right when you needed it. You'll be amazed at how quickly the pile of rocks disappears without you having to worry about them.

December 16

"Neither do people pour new wine into old wineskins. If they do, the skins will burst; the wine will run out and the wineskins will be ruined. No, they pour new wine into new wineskins, and both are preserved" (Matthew 9.17 NIV).

God did a new thing. Jesus came into the Earth to bring the New Wine of Grace to the world. This wine brings us true and eternal gladness, joy and peace. People tried for thousands of years to be perfect according to the Old Wine of the Law, and they failed miserably. The Law was a constant reminder that we needed a Savior. We can never be perfect. We can never reach God on our own. We need a Mediator to bridge the gap between us and God. Someone Who "may lay his hand on us both" (Job 9.33 NKJV).

Jesus' body became like the "wineskin," which carried the New Wine of Grace. By faith, we receive this New Wine, and we can finally have a relationship with God even in our imperfect state. Jesus supernaturally gave us His perfection and took our imperfection into the tomb where He left it. This New Wine should make us giddy with joy! We don't have to be good enough, wise enough or spiritual enough. Our striving has ended, and we can rest with Jesus in His perfection! Now our love and joy are what motivate us to want to please God, not fear and striving.

We rejoice because we live in the New Testament era where the New Wine of Christ flows freely. At any moment throughout the day, you can drink deeply from the wineskin of Christ and receive His peace by faith. We don't have to earn it. We will never lose it. All we have to do is believe and the Wine of Grace is ours, providing us with God's love, joy, peace and provision every day!

Joy ACTIVITY

Jesus wondered if He would "find faith on the earth" when He returns (Luke 18.8 NIV). The fundamental foundation of a relationship with God through Jesus Christ is faith. God extends His grace to us through Jesus, and we grab this grace with hands of faith. What exactly is faith? The Bible explains it this way: "Now faith is confidence in what we hope for and assurance about what we do not see" (Hebrews 11.1 NIV).

Life as a Christ-follower always entails faith. God gives us promises, and we believe them by faith, regardless of what our circumstances tell us. We are called to "live by faith, not sight" (2 Corinthians 5.7 NIV). If we can believe God for salvation through

Christ, we can believe God for every promise He gives us personally about our lives, relationships and situations.

Image that Jesus is standing in front of you, and He is asking you to make a list of what you are currently believing for by faith. Declare a verbal list of every promise that God has given you. Don't allow guilt or disbelief to enter into your speech. Make a bold declaration of each promise to God and put all your faith on the line. Believe that all your promises are "Yes" in Christ" (2 Corinthians 1.20 NIV).

December 17

"They devoted themselves to the apostles' teaching and to fellowship, to the breaking of bread and to prayer" (Acts 2.42 NIV).

Breaking bread with others became a huge theme for the followers of Jesus. The bread symbolizes Jesus' body and the sustenance and provision He gives us each day. Breaking bread with others carries with it a unique experience. There are some things we receive from God individually; however, there are other things we receive from God corporately. Therefore, breaking bread with other Christ-followers offers us ingredients that we cannot gain alone.

Every person has her or his own exclusive vantage point of Jesus. When we surround

70

ourselves with multiple vantage points of Jesus through the eyes of other Believers, we receive a more detailed understanding of and a deepened familiarity with Him. Sharing a meal with others is one of the best ways to exchange words, experiences and thoughts of God.

Plus, the Bible says that we overcome "...by the blood of the Lamb and by the word of their testimony..." (Revelation 12.11 NIV). There is "bread" in the testimonies of others that we can feed on and find strength in. The perspectives and experiences of others can help us overcome our own battles by seeing God move in their lives. We listen to stories of victory and words of wisdom, and our spirits gain courage to believe that there are no hopeless endings with God. Relationships take effort. Planning meals with others takes work. But we will find that the effort and work are worth the nutrients we receive in return.

Joy ACTIVITY

Plan a meal with other Christ-followers. Ask the Holy Spirit who you should invite. They can be old friends or new friends. They can be pastors at your church. Or they can be neighbors you would like to get to know. You can make the meal as extravagant or simple as you want but try to have the experience at your home. You can provide all the food or just the main dish and ask others to bring the sides. Whatever you do, the hardest step is to set the date and send out the invitation.

 Today, set the date and choose your guests. Breaking bread with others will truly bless you, and the effort will be well worth it. After your first meal, you may become so captivated with the experience that you decide to plan to break bread with others monthly or even weekly.

December 18

"Later, knowing that everything had now been finished, and so that Scripture would be fulfilled, Jesus said, 'I am thirsty.' A jar of wine vinegar was there, so they soaked a sponge in it, put the sponge on a stalk of the hyssop plant, and lifted it to Jesus' lips. When he had received the drink, Jesus said, 'It is finished.' With that, he bowed his head and gave up his spirit" (John 19.28-30 NIV).

Jesus said that He had water to give others that would completely eliminate thirst (John 4.14). However, when He went onto the cross, He cried out: "I am thirsty." Jesus took our sins on the cross, and the Living Water He carried was now diverted to us. For the first time, Jesus knew what it was to thirst because our sins He carried separated Him from God for a time. The Living Water flowing to Him from God's Spirit stopped, and He experienced the thirst for which people suffer who don't know God.

 When Jesus cried out for a drink, the guards below dipped a sponge into a vessel of wine vinegar or sour wine and gave it to Jesus. The sour wine represents the Old Wine of the Law. He drank this wine as a symbol that He was fulfilling the Law on our behalf. He was consuming the Law, so His blood could pour out Grace. After Jesus drank the sour wine, He proclaimed, "It is finished," and He died (John 19.29-30). The job of reconciling humanity back to God was finally done!

The Bible says that Jesus gave His life willingly for us, but He also has the authority to take it back up again (John 10.18). Jesus died carrying our sins into the tomb, and He rose again leaving our sin behind. Our sin is erased, and now we can have a relationship with a Holy God. Jesus consumed the Old Wine of the Law, so He could pour out His New Wine of Grace onto all creation.

Joy ACTIVITY

It is finished! Jesus took our sins, our need, our pain, our illness, our addictions and our heartbreak; and in return, He gave us His righteousness, His provision, His comfort, His healing, His freedom and His joy! Make a list of every struggle you are facing today. After you make your list, take a red pen, pencil or crayon and cross out each item in your list. Finally, in big words across the list write, "IT IS FINISHED!"

Jesus has taken everything on this list into the tomb and left it there. Now He blesses you from the overflow of His goodness and grace.

December 19

"Now he who supplies seed to the sower and bread for food will also supply and increase your store of seed and will enlarge the harvest of your righteousness" (2 Corinthians 9.10 NIV).

Sometimes there is bread that God wants to give us. However, other times God gives us the seeds to plant, sow and make into bread ourselves. Making our own bread (nutrients of Christ) is a powerful way to increase our storehouse of God's goodness in our hearts, minds and lives. There are times when God invites us to the feast, and there are other times God wants to produce and multiply a feast within us.

When God does this, it may feel like He is separating us from others for a time. Maybe He's moving us out from the comfortable wings of a large bread-producing ministry, so we can produce a unique bread of our own. We must remember that breaking is part of the process of multiplying. If we feel like God is breaking us, we must recognize that it is only to multiply us. When God multiplies the bread that He is producing within us, He is able to feed the people around us with this new bread. But we have to be willing to go through the process with Him.

If we don't trust God in the process, the bread He wants to create through us will never come to pass. How many people will be affected if we don't allow God to do this work in us? The world can be a place overflowing with the harvest of God if all His children would be used by Him to create distinctive loaves. Let us not only feast on bread, but let us also create bread in obedience to God with the helping hand of Jesus, Who gives us all the seeds and ingredients we need.

Joy ACTIVITY

Is God trying to give you seeds to create your own bread that represents the goodness of Jesus Christ? There are people all around you who will be blessed by what only you can create. Ask God today what it is He is trying to produce in you. Look through your pantry for any form of seeds. They can be corn seeds, sunflower seeds or nut seeds. Take a seed for each thing God wants to produce in your life. Bring those seeds outside and have a prayer time with God.

Tell God that you will trust Him with the process and bury each seed into the ground as a symbol that your heart is fertile soil for new growth. Later, when the process of producing a harvest becomes difficult, you can remember this day of planting and strengthen your resolve with faith.

December 20

"Instead, one of the soldiers pierced Jesus' side with a spear, bringing a sudden flow of blood and water" (John 19.34 NIV).

After Jesus consumed the sour wine and gave up His Spirit, one of the soldiers pierced Jesus' side—both blood and water poured out. Jesus' pierced side is an Old Testament prophecy and New Testament fulfillment of that prophecy (Zechariah 12.10). The symbolism of both blood and water pouring out gives us insight into the beauty found in such an ugly death. Finally, because Jesus paid the price for our sin, God's Living Water could flow freely over the Earth. Not only that, Jesus' blood (wine – the fruit of Living Water mixed with earth) is flowing freely, as well.

We have a double blessing. We have God's Spirit and Jesus' blood on Earth! All of creation has been reconciled back to the Father. Water cleanses and blood purifies. No sin, no matter how despicable, can stain our lives with that much holy pressure washing it clean! Every sin we have committed and every sin committed toward us have no hold over us. The blood and water are too powerful, and the shackles of shame and guilt are washed away in waves of grace and love.

Not only is the Living Water pouring over us, it is also springing up from within us. The more space we give God in our hearts, minds and lives, the more the River of Living Water will flow. Let us no longer hold onto to doubt, fear, shame, worry or mistrust. God loves us so much that He willingly died to have a relationship with us (Romans 5.8). Once we see how much we are truly loved, sin will no longer have a hold over us.

Joy ACTIVITY

The Bible says that God's compassion is new every morning (Lamentation 3.22-23). This means that Living Water of God and the blood of Jesus flow into each new day with all the mercy and favor we need to face that day's challenges and enjoy that day's blessing. God's supply of care and compassion is endless and can flow into even the tiniest corners of our lives.

 The candy cane can be a symbol of Living Water (white like snow) and Jesus' blood (red like wine) twisted together in one powerful New Testament statement of grace. Plan to make a batch of your favorite sugar cookies. You can buy a box of ready to make sugar cookies or use your own recipe. The only difference is you will frost these cookies with red and white frosting stripes to symbolize the water and blood that flowed for our salvation.

Red and White Frosting

- 3 cups of powdered sugar
- ½ cup softened butter
- 2 tsp vanilla extract
- 2 tablespoons of milk
- Red food coloring

Combine powdered sugar and softened butter with a mixer. Add vanilla and 2 tablespoons of milk and mix until smooth. Divide frosting in two separate bowls. Add red food coloring to one bowl and mix until the frosting is red. Place each portion of frosting into a food storage bag and twist and tie off the opening of the bag. Use scissors and cut one of the corners of the bag big enough to allow the frosting to create a thin line of frosting across. Frost each cookie with lines of white and red frosting.

December 21

"Which of you, if your son asks for
bread, will give him a stone? Or if he
asks for a fish, will give him a
snake? If you, then, though you are
evil, know how to give good gifts to
your children, how much more will
your Father in heaven give good
gifts to those who ask him!"
([Matthew 7.9-11 NIV](#)).

Sometimes, we don't receive because we
don't ask. Other times, we accept gifts
that are actually curses because we look to
others rather than God. The Bible says that
when we ask God for gifts according to His
will, He will provide because His will is always
for our good ([Jeremiah 29.11](#)). This doesn't
mean He'll provide right away. In fact, many
of God's blessings take time to finally arrive

in the natural, but we have to trust that they are there in the supernatural waiting for the right moment to spring up.

We can't give up waiting. We can't look to others for what only God can provide. During the season of waiting, we must do everything in our power to boost our faith. We can feed on the bread (sustenance) that God has for us each day, trusting that He will come through for us in His time. It may seem to linger, but God's promised gift to you will "certainly come" (Habakkuk 2.3 NIV).

Joy ACTIVITY

While doing your Christmas shopping, buy three extra gifts. Wrap each gift and place a tag on each box. On the tags write the following:

85

Jesus loves you. Here is a gift
that He wants you to have this
Christmas Season.
I pray it blesses you.
xoxo

Keep the three wrapped presents in your car
and ask the Holy Spirit to show you who to
give each present to during the next few
days. It may be a barista at the coffee shop
drive-thru. It may a teller at the bank. It may
be someone waiting at the bus stop.
Whoever it is, he or she will be blessed with
a special gift from God through your
faithfulness.

December 22

"Wine that gladdens human hearts, oil to make their faces shine, and bread that sustains their hearts" (Psalm 104.15 NIV).

The bread of God sustains us, but it is the Wine of Jesus that gladdens our hearts. Bread gives us what we need to survive, but the wine is poured out in celebration. In the Bible, Jesus is compared to the Bridegroom and we are His Bride (Revelation 19.7 NIV). God is preparing His Bride to meet Jesus face-to-face when He returns. As we wait, we can become giddy with anticipation. We are going to be with Jesus in Heaven where this is no more pain and no more sorrow (Revelation 21.4)

Jesus did all the work to make us a stunning and perfect bride. His Finished Work on the Cross wiped away all our blemishes, and we are now glowing with innocent beauty! The same goes with those around us who have accepted Jesus as their Lord and Savior. They too are stunning beauties in God's eyes. That is why we want to see the best in them because that is what God sees. It is so much easier to love others when we see them through the eyes of God.

 It is time! The wedding feast has been arranged. The date is set. The invitations have been sent out. Jesus has already poured out the New Wine in preparation for the wedding feast. Our hearts are to be glad and our spirits should lift up in expectation. He is coming soon. We don't know exactly when—*but, suddenly*—He will come and

sweep us off our feet and bring us home to His heavenly palace ([Matthew 24.36](#)).

I magine a richly adorned grand table that is set and ready for your wedding with the Bridegroom in Heaven. The seats are occupied by family and friends whom you dearly loved on Earth. Who do you envision joining you at the wedding feast? Thank God for every familiar face that you see. Are there faces that are missing? Which friends and family in your life haven't accepted Jesus as their Lord and Savior?

Today, why not share with those you love who don't know Jesus about why you love Him. Explain that Jesus died for our sins, so we could have a relationship with God now and forever. Let them know that you care about them and desire to see their face in Heaven with you.

December 23

"Because there is one loaf, we, who are many, are one body, for we all share the one loaf" (1 Corinthians 10.17 NIV).

The Bible says that all Christ-followers become as one Body, a single Bride, awaiting her Bridegroom (Romans 12.5). We all share the "loaf" of Christ, and His nutrients translate in unique ways within each of us. We were created to need others. We only know in part, and we gain a better perspective when our walk of faith involves other people. Church is the single best way to surround ourselves with other Believers. Church can happen in a building, in homes, in offices, in schools, at concerts or wherever Christ is shared. We limit God's powerful flow when we try to define where He can move.

Jesus said that "...where two or three gather in my name, there am I with them" (Matthew 18.20 NIV). Jesus is there with us. We can do church at any time of day and at any place. When we meet an old friend at the mall who needs prayer, we can do church there. When we are at the office and there is a difficult problem that doesn't seem to have an answer, we can do church there. When a family member is having a tough day, we can do church there. And when a stranger passes us by on the street and God tells us to speak, we can do church there, as well.

We are all one Body, so shouldn't we be looking for ways to improve our body and to keep it healthy and strong? Let us replace accusation with encouragement, doubt with belief, fear with prayer, jealousy with admiration and hate with love. Every life-giving interaction we have with people will deposit a loaf of Christ in them. The world would change for good if we simply offered the bread of Christ to everyone we meet!

Joy ACTIVITY

Think back to your interactions and conversations that you have had with others. Is there a need that you can fill? Is there a loaf of Christ that you can offer to someone you care about? Does a co-worker need help replacing a part on her or his car? Is there a single mother who would love for you to watch her kids, so she can go Christmas shopping? Is there a young man who doesn't have a home to go to for Christmas dinner? Is there someone in your life to who you need to impart a special blessing?

Ask the Holy Spirit who He wants you to bless and how. He is a Good Father, and He wants to bless others through you. He will show you exactly who you can touch with the love of Christ this Christmas season.

December 24

"For my flesh is real food and my blood is real drink. Whoever eats my flesh and drinks my blood remains in me, and I in them. Just as the living Father sent me and I live because of the Father, so the one who feeds on me will live because of me. This is the bread that came down from heaven. Your ancestors ate manna and died, but whoever feeds on this bread will live forever" (John 6.55-58 NIV).

Just like Jesus, we are both physical and spiritual beings. However, only when the physical reality of our lives is submitted to the spiritual reality will we be fully engaged in the "real" life that God has for us. Jesus calls His body "real" food and His blood "real" drink because they are of a spiritual nature. They are the supernatural nourishment that our spirits crave. Without Jesus, our spirits are dead. But through Him, our spirits are born to new life. Our food requirements for this life, though, don't end at being born again (John 3.3).

If Jesus simply wanted to give us salvation, He would take us right to Heaven after we accept Him as Lord and Savior. However, Jesus has more for us to do in this world. God has a plan and purpose for our lives on Earth, and we are becoming the people we will be for eternity. We will need to come to the table of God and eat the "real" food of Jesus to become strong enough and persevere long enough to achieve our destiny.

Joy ACTIVITY

Ask yourself if you think you are getting enough "real" food and "real" drink from Christ. If not, will you make a few adjustments to your daily routine in order to feed your spirit well? Here are a few simple suggestions:

- Download Christian Podcasts and Bible Apps on your phone, so at any time you can feast on the bread and wine of Jesus.
- Wake up fifteen minutes earlier every morning in order to have some quiet time with the Lord.
- Take a nightly bath away from electronics where you can pray.
- Look through your bookshelves and take out any Christian books you have purchased but forgot to read. Place them on your nightstand and try to read a chapter every night.

- Invite a friend you admire for her or his walk of faith to lunch. Try to keep a monthly meeting with that person.
- Start attending church. If you already attend, volunteer to serve.
- Listen to encouraging Christian music while driving, working out or sitting at your desk. You'll be surprised at how the words of life with lift your spirit.
- Take daily walks where you can talk with the Lord and listen to His voice.
- Memorize Bible verses that inspire and uplift you.
- Keep a thankful heart. Focus on your blessings more than your struggles and offer up continual thanksgiving to God.

December 25

"While they were eating, Jesus took bread, and when he had given thanks, he broke it and gave it to his disciples, saying, 'Take and eat; this is my body' Then he took a cup, and when he had given thanks, he gave it to them, saying, 'Drink from it, all of you. This is my blood of the covenant, which is poured out for many for the forgiveness of sins'" (Matthew 26.26-28 NIV).

At the Last Supper in the Upper Room with His disciples, Jesus set a precedent: communion. We partake in communion to remember why Jesus was born and why He died. Through His body (bread) and blood (wine), our sins have been forgiven forever, and we can now have a relationship with a Holy God on Earth. This relationship continues after our bodies die, and we come face-to-face with God in Heaven. If we haven't accepted Jesus as our Lord and Savior, we can't have a relationship with a Holy God on Earth; and when our bodies die, our lack of relationship continues, and we are separated from God in hell.

Two distinct eternities that are vastly different. Heaven is the presence of God, and hell is the absence of God. Jesus says, "I am the way and the truth and the life. No one comes to the Father except through me" (John 14.6 NIV).

The only way we can be with God in Heaven for eternity is to accept salvation through Jesus Christ. Jesus did all the work. All we have to do is receive this Great Gift that God has given us. It is literally gifted wrapped with a big bow with our name on it. All we have to do is open it!

If you haven't accepted Jesus into your heart, why not receive this Great Gift today? You can celebrate being reborn on the most special day of the year: Christmas! The Bible says that all you have to do in order to receive the gift of salvation is to declare and believe:

> "If you declare with your mouth, 'Jesus is Lord,' and believe in your heart that God raised him from the dead, you will be saved" (Romans 10.9 NIV).

Speak the following words aloud or silently and believe in your heart.

"Dear, Jesus. I want the gift of salvation through the body You broke and the blood

You poured out on my behalf. Come into my heart, Jesus. I make you the Lord over my life. I want to have a relationship with God, and I ask the Holy Spirit to make a home in my life. Thank you, Jesus, for dying for me. I want to live with God for eternity in Heaven. I pray this in Jesus' name, Amen."

Christmas Communion

Now it is time to get your Eucharist elements (Bread and Juice/Wine), so you can partake in Christmas Communion. This book includes a bread and juice recipe if you would like to make homemade communion elements for your communion celebration. If not, you can purchase bread and juice/wine from the grocery store or use what you have at home.

You can partake in Christmas Communion during your holiday meal or you can simply add it to your Christmas festivities. You can even bring Christmas Communion wherever you go! Remember, when you eat the bread, you envision Jesus' broken body that was multiplied on Earth to provide us everything we need to live a life pleasing to Him. And when you drink the juice, you envision Jesus' blood poured out onto the Earth to forgive our sins and reconcile us back to God.

Rejoice today! We live in the New Testament era that the Old Testament prophets could only dream about!

Joy ACTIVITY

Take your bread and juice and stand before your Christmas tree. If you are with family and friends, have everyone make a circle around the Christmas tree holding their piece of bread and cup of juice. Another  metaphor for Jesus in the Bible is the Tree of Life, and your Christmas tree can be symbolic of His presence in the room

(Revelation 22.2). Hold up the bread and say, "This is the Bread of Christ. Name one gift that Jesus has given you this Christmas season." Take turns and let everyone explain one gift that Jesus has given them. Then ask everyone to eat the bread.

Next, hold up the cup of juice and say, "This is the Wine of Christ. Reflect on Jesus' forgiveness for your sins and take a moment to thank Him silently for giving you His righteousness, so you can have a relationship with a Holy God." Allow for a minute of silence. Finally, ask everyone to drink the juice.

Then offer up a prayer or you can recite the prayer below.

"Father, thank You for sending Jesus to die on the cross for our sins, so we could live forever in Heaven with You. This Christmas, we recognize that the Greatest Gift under the tree is the gift of Your Son. He gave up His holy robes to be born in a manger. He gave

up His rightful place at Your throne, so He would walk this Earth with us. Through Jesus, we are never alone. Thank You, God, for creating us. Thank You, Jesus, for dying for us. And thank You, Holy Spirit, for living within us. We eat the Bread and drink the Wine of Christ, overflowing with feelings of faith, honor and awe of Your sacrifice for us. We pray this in Jesus' name, Amen."

Bread Recipe

NEWLYWED BREAD

1 c. warm water
1 pkg yeast
2 T. sugar
2 1/2 c. flour
1 t. salt
1 egg beaten
2 T. olive oil

Dissolve yeast in warm water. Stir in sugar and salt; add half of the flour. Add oil and egg. Beat until smooth, while adding remaining flour. Cover and let rise in a warm place 30 minutes.

Grease an 8 1/2 x 4 1/2 x 2 1/2. Stir (punch) down dough and spoon into pan, filling half full. Let rise 20-30 minutes more. Bake at 400 degrees for 18-20 minutes. Serves 8.

Bread recipe by Holly Smith.
https://hishollysmith.org/.

Juice Recipe

CHRISTMAS VINE JUICE

Pick or purchase four pounds of Concord, Niagara or Delaware grapes or grapes of your choice.

Equipment:

A strainer
1 large basin
1 masher
1 large 6 or 8-quart cooking pot
A large, fine mesh sieve or cheesecloth

Put grapes in large cooking pot and add water. Wash each grape, pulling it from the stem, and discard shriveled grapes. Pour water out and mash grapes until juices begin to flow.

Place cooking pot with mashed grapes and juices onto the stove burner. Cook on medium heat until grape juice begins to lightly bubble and mash once more to release additional juices.

Turn heat to simmer and let juice cook for ten more minutes, stirring occasionally to prevent grapes from sticking to the bottom of the pot. Turn off the heat and let the mashed grapes cool.

Place the mesh sieve or two layers of cheesecloth over the large basin. Use a rubber band or tied cord to keep cheesecloth in place. Pour the cooled, mashed grapes over the sieve or cheesecloth. Juices will flow through, leaving mashed grapes behind.

Enjoy the juice and discard the mashed grape skins or use for compost.

Juice recipe by Alisa Hope Wagner.
https://alisahopewagner.com

Meet Alisa

Alisa Hope Wagner writes words of inspiration and imagination. She's been married to her high school sweetheart for over twenty years, and together they raise their two sons and daughter in a Christ-centered home. She has a bachelor's degree in English and a master's degree in English Applied Linguistics. She has taught Bible studies, led discipleship small groups and lectured at churches, schools and universities.

Alisa is an international award-winning author of both fiction and non-fiction books. She has been in two reality TV shows, competed and placed in bodybuilding competitions and won an MMA fight by TKO in a little over a minute. She is co-founder and editor of enLIVEn Devotionals that publishes award-winning anthologies that support world missions. She has written and published over thirty fiction and nonfiction books, which can be found on her Amazon Page and Audible Page.